MW01140318

Meet Christopher

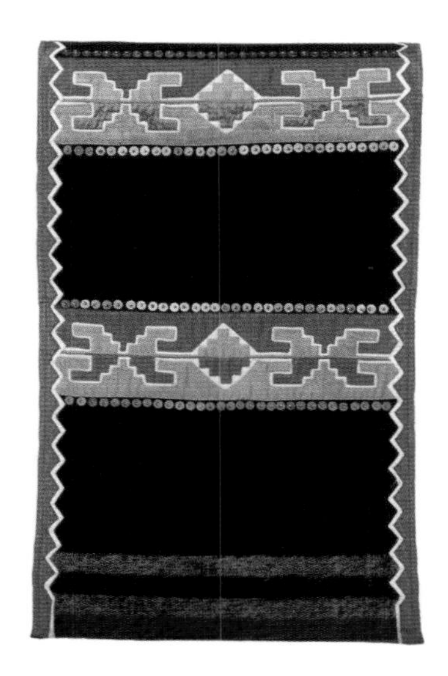

For my sister, Annie; the best teacher I know.
—GMS

Council Oak Books, 2105 E. 15th St., Suite B, Tulsa, OK 74104

Project Director and Head of Publications, NMAI: Terence Winch

Series Editor, NMAI: Sally Barrows

Series Design Concept: Andrea L. Boven, Boven Design Studio, Inc.

Book Design: Carl Brune

The National Museum of the American Indian is committed to advancing knowledge and understanding of the Native cultures of the Western Hemisphere—past, present, and future—through partnership with Native people and others. The museum works to support the continuance of culture, traditional values, and transitions in contemporary Native life. The museum's publishing program seeks to augment awareness of Native American beliefs and lifeways, and educate the public about the history and significance of Native cultures.

For information about the Smithsonian's National Museum of the American Indian, visit the NMAI website at www.AmericanIndian.si.edu.

To support the museum by becoming a member, call 1-800-242-NMAI (6624) or click on "Membership & Giving" on the website.

On the half-title page: Folded wool trailer, decorated using a special technique called ribbonwork. A trailer hangs from a dancer's waist, falling behind his back legs nearly to the ground. This one, which includes a lightning-pattern border, was probably made in the early 1900s. (NMAI S7529)

First edition

10 9 8 7 6 5 4 3 2 1

Library of Congress Cataloging-in-Publication Data
Simermeyer, Genevieve.
Meet Christopher : an Osage Indian boy from Oklahoma / Genevieve Simermeyer ; with photographs by Katherine Fogden. -- 1st ed.
p. cm. -- (My world: young Native Americans today ; 4)
ISBN 978-1-57178-217-5 (hardcover : alk. paper) 1. Cote, Christopher. 2. Osage Indians--Biography--Juvenile literature. 3. Indian children--Oklahoma--Biography--Juvenile literature. 4. Osage Indians--Social life and customs--Juvenile literature. I. National Museum of the American Indian (U.S.) II. Title.
E99.O8C677 2008
978.004'9752--dc22 2008015079
[B]

Meet Christopher

An Osage Indian Boy from Oklahoma

Genevieve Simermeyer
With photographs by Katherine Fogden

My World: Young Native Americans Today

Smithsonian
National Museum of the American Indian

in Association with

Council
Oak Books

Tulsa / San Francisco

Ha we! My name is Genevieve Simermeyer, but a lot of people call me Jennie. I was named after my great-grandmother. I have many different cultures in my background, including Scottish, Norwegian, German, Irish, and Native American. My Native American heritage comes from my mother. Our tribe is called Osage, and I am a member of the Deer Clan. My Osage name is Wah-zha-zhi Me-tse-kee (pronounced: wa-SHA-she ME-sheh-key). This means "Sacred Osage Woman" and is a name often given to the first-born daughter of the Deer Clan.

I was born in Santa Fe, New Mexico, but I've also lived in other places, mainly Colorado. Today, I live in Maryland with my husband, Sequoyah.

I have two brothers, Jonathan and Benjamin, and one sister named Anne. Although we all grew up in Colorado, our parents took us to Oklahoma for a few weeks every June when we were young to visit relatives and participate in the Osage dances. Now that we are grown up, we still go to Oklahoma every year in June, and we bring our own families.

Osage people haven't always gone by that name. According to one Osage story, the people started as two separate groups—Tzi-sho (pronounced: SEE-sho), or Sky People, and Hun-ka, or Earth People. The Earth People were divided into two groups: Water People, who were called Wa-zha-zhi, and Land People, who were called Hunka. When French traders first made contact with Osage people, they encountered a group of the Wa-zha-zhi (Water People). "Osage" is the way the French traders pronounced the word "Wa-zha-zhi." They ended up calling all of the Sky and Earth people "Osage." Today, we call ourselves Osage or Wa-zha-zhi.

GEORGE CATLIN. *An Osage Indian Lancing a Buffalo,* 1846–1848. OIL ON CANVAS, 49.7 X 70 CM. (SMITHSONIAN AMERICAN ART MUSEUM, 1985.66.587)

PHOTO BY MARK R. HARRINGTON. (NMAI N2754)

PHOTO BY MARK R. HARRINGTON. (NMAI N2755)

TOP: The bent-sapling frame of a traditional Osage lodge, 1908. **BOTTOM:** A similar lodge, covered with canvas, 1908.

The Osage reservation is in the northeastern corner of Oklahoma, but this is not where Osage people originally came from. Before Europeans came to this land, Osage people occupied a very large territory in the eastern Plains. Originally, Osages were part of a larger group that included four other tribes—Kaw, Omaha, Ponca, and Quapaw. Eventually, the five groups separated, and the Osages settled in the Missouri River Valley.

Most tribes in the Plains lived in tipis, but the Osage people lived in rectangular lodges that were covered with bark, woven mats, or hides. People stayed in these lodges during the planting and harvesting seasons. When they left their villages during hunting seasons, people took down the coverings but left the pole frames. During that time, families lived in hunting camps, where their houses were more like tents. Osage people mainly hunted buffalo, deer, elk, and sometimes bears. They gathered wild foods such as cherries, plums, pecans, walnuts, and different kinds of berries. They also had gardens where they grew corn, beans, and squash that could be dried and saved to eat throughout the year.

This map shows the extent of Osage lands before Europeans arrived. Most Osages lived for part of the year in villages near the Missouri and Osage rivers, but their hunting territory covered a wide area that includes parts of four present-day states.

Between 1808 and 1865, the Osages, like many other Native people, signed treaties with the United States government in which they agreed to give up vast amounts of their territory. They hoped this would help them to live in peace. They moved to a reservation (an area set aside specifically for Native Americans) in southeastern Kansas in the 1830s. As more white settlers and other Indian tribes moved west, Osage leaders gave up more land. By the early 1870s, the United States offered to pay the Osage Tribe ten million dollars to move completely and make more space for the newcomers. In 1873 the Osage purchased the land in Indian Territory that is now known as the Osage Reservation.

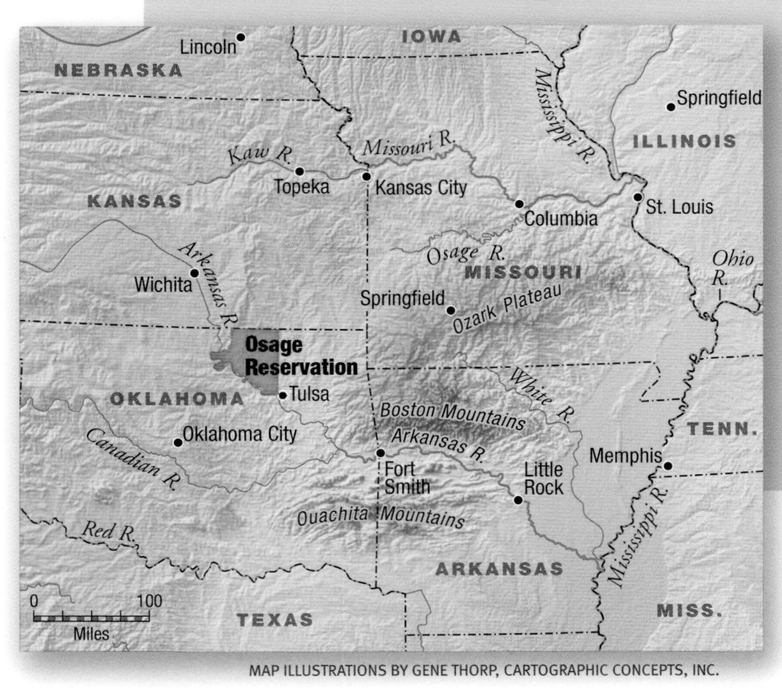

MAP ILLUSTRATIONS BY GENE THORP, CARTOGRAPHIC CONCEPTS, INC.

Many different Native American tribes were moved to Indian Territory, which is now the state of Oklahoma. Today, almost forty different tribes are located in Oklahoma. Even though a lot of Osage people don't live in Oklahoma or on the Osage reservation, Osages are one of the largest tribes in the state.

The shaded area in this map shows the Osage Nation Reservation (also called Osage County) in Oklahoma today.

Jennie's grandmother, Georgeann Gray (the littlest girl in the middle, in a white dress), and Christopher's great-grandmother, Louise Gray (also in a white dress, sitting in the front), were sisters. Their mother's name was Jennie, too. She is the only person in this picture who is not wearing modern clothing. This family photo was probably taken in 1920. (COURTESY OF KATHRYN RED CORN.)

I would like to introduce you to my cousin, Christopher. Even though we're cousins, Christopher calls me "Aunt Jennie" because I am older than he is. In the same way, I call his grandmother Aunt Kathryn, even though she is really my mom's cousin. In the Osage way, the terms *aunt* or *uncle* can be used for someone who may not actually be your parents' brother or sister. It's done to show respect and to give the older person the responsibility of looking out for the younger one, as any aunt or uncle would. Let's go meet Christopher, and he'll help you learn more about his life as an Osage boy.

Ha we! My name is Christopher Cote (pronounced: ko-TAY). I am eleven years old and in the sixth grade. I'm a member of the Eagle Clan of the Osage Nation of Oklahoma. I have three brothers. Geoffrey is older, and Andrew and David are both younger than me. We live in a town called Skiatook (pronounced: SKY-tuke). Skiatook is right on the edge of the Osage reservation. I have lived in Skiatook since I was four years old.

I'm like a lot of other kids my age. I love to be outside and play with my brothers and friends. Bike riding is one of our favorite activities, but we also play tag, build forts, or just hang out. In the summer, we like to go swimming to keep cool because it can get pretty hot in Oklahoma. I also like movies, especially the *Lord of the Rings* series. My parents give me chores such as folding the laundry, washing the dinner dishes, and watching after my younger brothers.

Christopher and his family after church. Left to right: Christopher's dad; his middle brother, Andrew; his mom; his youngest brother, David; Christopher; and his oldest brother, Geoffrey.

My mom is Osage, and she grew up on our reservation. My mom and dad met in college. My dad is Native American, too—his tribes are from the northeast part of the United States. He is Iroquois and Penobscot. Penobscots are from Maine—which is a long way from Oklahoma! When I was in second grade we drove to Maine for Christmas to visit Grandma, Uncle Ray, and Uncle Matt. It was a long trip, and the snow was like a huge white blanket on everything. It was the most snow I've ever seen in my whole life!

Geoffrey, Andrew, Christopher, and David take their bikes out of the backyard shed for a ride after school.

A road on the outskirts of Pawhuska, surrounded by cow pastures.

Highway 20 is the road between Pawhuska and Skiatook, where Christopher lives with his parents and brothers. Here, the highway crosses Skiatook Lake.

Another reason I like living in Oklahoma is because this is where my *i'ko* (pronounced: EE-ko) lives. *I'ko* is the Osage word for grandmother. We go visit my i'ko a lot, especially when we don't have school, because she lives only about forty-five minutes away. Her house is in the town of Pawhuska, on the Osage reservation. It is fun to visit her because she has a huge yard where there is a lot of room for my brothers, me, and our cousins to play. Sometimes in the summer, I'ko lets us camp out in the yard, in a tent on her big lawn. What I like most about sleeping outside is listening to the coyotes. They don't scare me, but I can tell how close they are by how loudly they howl. Sometimes, though, all I hear is traffic from the main road. The worst part about camping is that it can get pretty hot, even at night, but I think it's worth it.

In the summer, Christopher and his brothers sometimes sleep in a tent outside their grandmother's house in Pawhuska. The tent they use is the yellow and orange one on the left.

I'ko is good to talk to. She makes sure my brothers and I learn about Osage people and customs. She tells us stories about what things were like for her growing up. My favorite story is about a tornado that came through Pawhuska when she was a baby and blew down the whole house around her. But she was okay! I'ko teaches us about our Osage family tree and helps with Osage language practice. She tells me and my brothers to be proud of who we are. My i'ko works at the Osage Tribal Museum. Every once in a while we go to the museum with her, where there are thousands of old pictures of Osage people. I even saw a picture of I'ko as a young girl, taken the year she had the honor of being named Osage Princess.

Skiatook is a small town, but it's growing. About six thousand people live here. Not everyone who lives in Skiatook is Indian, but some of the other families are Osage, too. Northeast Oklahoma is very beautiful. There are green trees, rolling hills, lakes, creeks, and a lot of pastureland used for raising cattle and horses. The fields and woods shelter wild animals, too, such as armadillos, raccoons, skunks, coyotes, and deer.

Christopher's grandmother at her desk at the Osage Tribal Museum in Pawhuska. She is the director of the museum, which opened in 1938 and has more than six thousand objects in its collection.

Christopher and his *i'ko* (grandmother) on the steps of her back porch in Pawhuska.

The museum is collecting as many photographs of Osage people as it can. This drawer in Christopher's grandmother's office is full of historic photos, including one of Bacon Rind (center), who was the principal chief of the Osage Tribe in the early 1900s.

Christopher in his music class. Behind him, left to right: Brandon Baker, Zachary Williams, the band's director, Mr. Allen, and Erin Tubby. Front row, left to right: David Peters, Christopher, and Omar Rendon.

This year, I started middle school, so now I'm in the same school as my older brother, Geoffrey. I even have some of the same teachers who taught him last year. The biggest change in sixth grade is switching classrooms for each subject. In grade school, I stayed in the same classroom all year. Now I take English, reading, math, science, and social studies—each with a different teacher. In middle school we don't have recess, which is okay with me. Recess was getting boring, and most of my new classes are fun.

In school, I like learning about history. I like all kinds of history, and I think it's cool to know about the past. I like learning about Indians, and also about how people from other parts of the world came to live in America.

During his careers class, Christopher talks about his i'ko and her work at the tribal museum.

I don't really know what I want to be when I get older, but I might become a historian. It would be pretty fun to work in a museum, like I'ko does. Math is one subject that I don't like as much because it can be so complicated. But I try hard in math because I know it's valuable. If I want to go to college to become a historian someday, I'll have to know how to do math!

I joined the band this year, and I'm learning to play the trombone. It takes a lot of work to make sure I play the right notes. I practice every day after school because I want to keep my spot in the band.

One of my favorite activities outside of school is Osage language class. I go to language class at the public library one evening a week with my mom, dad, and Geoffrey. The class is special because I am learning a language that could disappear soon if no one works to keep it going. About 130 years ago, Osage children—like other Native kids—were sent away from their families to live at boarding schools, where they were supposed to speak only English. Over time, a lot of people forgot their language. Most boarding schools for Native children were shut down by the 1930s, but today not many people can speak Osage fluently. In my family, people stopped speaking it when I'ko's grandmother died. Her mom was still a little girl when her grandfather told all of his children that they needed to learn to speak English, since they didn't have a mother to take care of them anymore.

Osage students in an Osage language class at the Skiatook Library listen to the teacher pronounce numbers in Osage. Back row, left to right: Monte Ray Robedeaux, Jr., and Angela Pelayo. Front row, left to right: Isaac Pelayo, Gabriel Pelayo, Patricia Pratt, and Sam Evanoff.

Christopher's mom copies the Osage word for the color blue during language class. In Osage, blue is *ni ha do ho ecko* (pronounced: nee-ha-DOH-ho-eck-oh), spelled ʎ∩-√Λ ƊO-√O α-ɮO in Osage characters. Translated directly, the syllables together mean "the color of water."

Some of the words and phrases I've learned are:

How are you?: 𐓈𐒰^.𐒹𐒷 𐓁𐒻^.𐒼𐓇𐒷
(pronounced: dan-HEH-neen-ksheh)

Good: 𐓍𐒰.𐒿𐒻 (pronounced: THA-dleh)

I don't know: 𐒻.𐓄𐒰.𐒹𐓂 𐓀𐒰^.𐓓𐒻
(pronounced: ee-puh-ho-MA-zhee)

Morning: 𐒼𐒰.𐓓𐒻 (pronounced: KAN-zhee)

Turtle: 𐒼𐒷 (pronounced: KEH)

Eagle: 𐒹𐓎.𐓍𐒰 (pronounced: HOO-thlaw)

Deer: 𐓈𐒰 (pronounced: DAW or TAW)

Dog: 𐓇𐓂^.𐒼𐒷 (pronounced: SHON-keh)

Red: 𐓓𐓎.𐓊𐒷 (pronounced: ZHOO-tseh)

Green: 𐓀𐒰.𐒹𐒻^ 𐓈𐓂.𐒹𐓂 𐒷.𐒼𐓂^
(pronounced: mah-HEE-do-ho-ekon)

Yellow: 𐓒𐒻 (pronounced: ZEE)

Christopher takes notes while his language teacher explains the sounds for some of the different symbols in the Osage language. Because the Osage language is written in a different alphabet than English, note-taking is especially important for remembering which letters correspond to the different sounds. For example, the symbol 𐒹 stands for the English *h* sound.

Today, our tribe is working to help people begin to speak our language again. One of our teachers, Mr. Lookout, told us that we are pioneers in re-learning Osage. Our class has people of all ages in it—kids, teenagers, adults, and elders—and all of us are excited to be learning our original language.

I think the Osage language sounds beautiful. And, it's interesting to listen to people speak it, to try to pick out words that I understand. I try to practice the words I've learned, but most other people, such as kids at school, can't understand what I'm saying. If I could, I would go to language class more than once a week, because then I would have more chances to practice. Instead, I repeat new words with my family. I hope to be fluent in Osage someday. Mr. Lookout said that he's been working at it for more than thirty years!

In the class, I'm also learning to write in Osage. Native American people used to have languages that were not written. Instead, they would draw pictures or symbols. Today, the Osage tribe has developed a mixture of symbols and letters to write our language.

After loading their supplies into the trailer, Christopher and friends from his patrol are excited about leaving for camp. Left to right: Joshua Keen, Kenny Giles, Christopher, and Nicholas Klein.

Being in the Boy Scouts is a big part of my life. I started when I was in first grade and just moved up from Cub Scouts last year. My brother Geoffrey and I are in the same troop, but not the same patrol. A patrol is a smaller group of kids who work together when we go camping. Camping is one of my favorite parts of scouting. I get to spend a lot of time outside and earn merit badges at the same time. So far, I've earned badges in mammal study, basketry, and leatherwork. My biggest goal in scouting is to make it to Eagle Scouts, the highest rank. To become a good Eagle Scout, I'll have to earn every merit badge possible by the time I'm eighteen. This would be a big honor, but I have a long road ahead of me.

Christopher and Geoffrey get a ride to the campground with their troop leader.

Christopher and Andrew sit on a rock outcrop overlooking Skiatook Lake while Christopher waits to hook a fish. Andrew is still learning to fish, and watching Christopher helps him.

When I'm not in school, I really like to go fishing with my dad and Geoffrey. Since my dad is from Maine, where there are lots of places to fish, he learned when he was a little boy. Now he teaches Geoffrey and me. We don't go out in a boat but instead stand on the shore. We like to use live bait, usually minnows. Sometimes it can be hard to bait the hook, but I'm getting pretty good at it. I've also learned how to cast the line. I think the fish we catch in Oklahoma are different from what my dad used to catch in Maine as a kid. Usually we get crappie, bass, or sometimes catfish. I caught a catfish once, on a field trip with my class, but I had to throw it back because it wasn't big enough to keep. When Andrew and David get older, I'll help them learn how to fish. Then, we can all four go together!

Skiatook Lake was created when the Skiatook Dam was built in 1977. These are the trunks of the trees that covered the landscape before the area was flooded to build the lake. This year, many more of them than usual rise above the surface because a long drought has made the lake shallower.

Christopher, Andrew, and their dad prepare their fishing poles with line and bait, but they get distracted when Geoffrey pretends to fall into the lake.

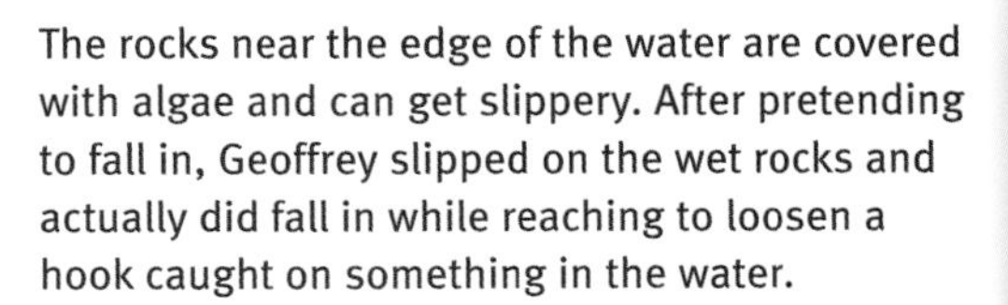

The rocks near the edge of the water are covered with algae and can get slippery. After pretending to fall in, Geoffrey slipped on the wet rocks and actually did fall in while reaching to loosen a hook caught on something in the water.

Christopher's dad jokes around in a buffalo hat while Christopher makes goulash for dinner.

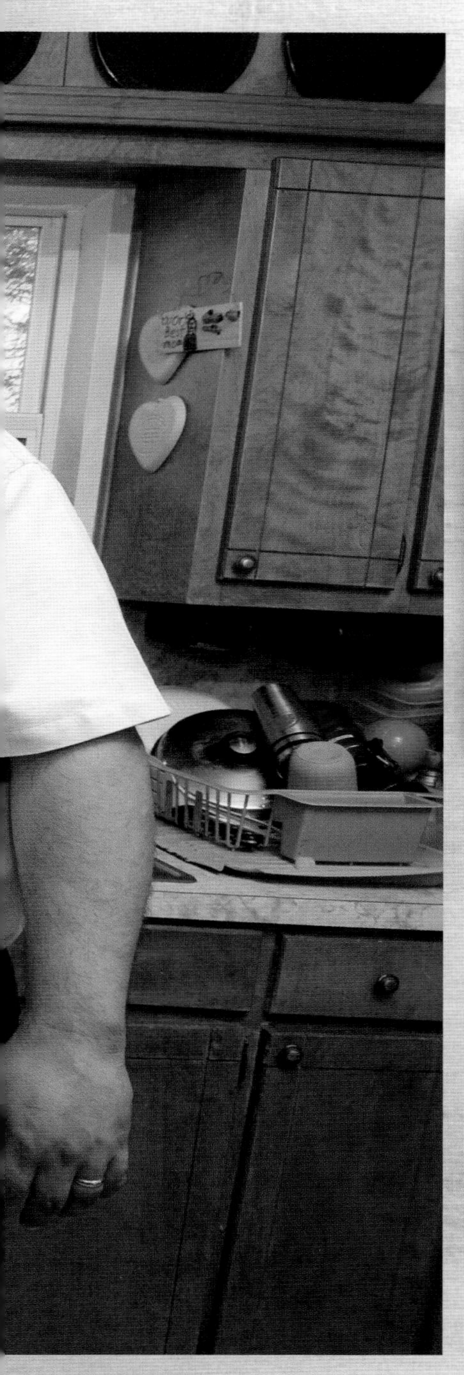

Christopher pours sauce over cooked noodles. The pan is heavy, so sometimes not all of the sauce makes it into the pot.

My dad also likes to cook—that's another thing he's teaching me. Whenever he cooks, one of my brothers or I usually help him. He knows how to make a lot of really good foods and desserts. My favorite is chicken alfredo with pasta. I'm still trying to learn all of the ingredients, but it sure tastes good when we're done! Cooking is hard because, if you mess up, you can't always undo your mistakes. My dad tells me that the best way to keep from messing up is to not take a break. I believe him because he has been cooking for fifteen years, and he's an awesome cook!

One of my specialties is called goulash. I love to make it because it's easy and we all like it. If I am in charge of cooking at Boy Scouts, I always make goulash! Here's what I put in it: short noodles (I like the twisty kind), ground hamburger, tomato sauce, Italian seasoning, and Parmesan cheese.

Christopher at his church with other Team Xtreme kids before they practice their dramas. Left to right: Christopher, Sawyer Hulslander, Skylar Hulslander, Natalie Hudson, Bailey Hulslander, and Samantha Hakanson.

Even though many Native American people participate in the traditional religions of their tribes, many do not. Historically the U.S. government suppressed, and even outlawed, Native American ceremonies. Many people were forced to convert to Christianity, and many people chose to convert. Either way, conversion was an attempt to have Native Americans assimilate, or blend in more, with white culture. Native American people today practice many kinds of religions or spiritual traditions. Many Indian families, like Christopher's, have been Christian for generations. Some people have combined their traditional cultural beliefs with Christianity, and some have adapted their tribal traditions to today's world.

For this Team Xtreme drama, Christopher plays the part of a look-out during a bank robbery. Behind him, Skylar Hulslander and Jordon Overton play the robbers.

Chris and the other "bank robbers" haul away the loot. Left to right: Billy Coover, Christopher, Skylar Hulslander, and Jordon Overton.

Another big part of my life is church. My family spends a lot of time on church activities. Almost every week, we have big gatherings and meals at the church. When I was in elementary school, I was a member of the kids' choir, but now that I'm older, I am in the youth drama group called Team Xtreme. Team Xtreme is fun because both middle school and high school kids are involved. We are kind of like storytellers. Our main purpose is to tell stories by performing short plays that teach lessons from the Bible.

We meet once a week, playing games and having a snack together before rehearsing. Most of the time, we perform for members of the church, but sometimes other people come to watch, too. Being with my friends during practice helps me to be less nervous when we're in front of an audience.

Osage delegation to Washington, D.C., 1906. Left to right, standing: Eaves Tall-Chief, Wah-she-hah (Bacon Rind), Bone Heart. Left to right, sitting: O-tha-xa-the (Well to Follow), Mi kc wa tha ka (Solitary Sun), He-ska-moie (Follower).

PHOTO BY DE LANCEY W. GILL. (SMITHSONIAN INSTITUTION NATIONAL ANTHROPOLOGICAL ARCHIVES NEGATIVE 4153)

When the Osage people moved for the final time, to their reservation in Oklahoma, it was not the end of trouble with their land. Osage people had always lived communally, with no one person owning the land. The United States government, however, wanted to divide up, or allot, all of the Indian reservation lands in the country. In 1887, Congress created a law called the Dawes Allotment Act. It stated that each member of each Indian tribe would receive a 160-acre section of the reservation for farming or raising livestock. All of the land not given to tribal members would be sold to white settlers. But full-time farming on a single piece of land was not a lifestyle that most American Indians knew, especially the Osages.

Osage leaders fought against the Dawes Act by going to Washington, D.C., and asking Congress to change the law. These leaders were able to delay the division of the Osage reservation for nineteen years. In 1906, a special allotment act was passed just for Osages. It saved all of their reservation lands without leaving any "leftover" land for outsiders. Each tribal member was allotted 658 acres. The 1906 act also reserved a communal area, known as the Indian Village, in each of the reservation's three districts—Pawhuska, Hominy, and Grayhorse. The Indian Villages are the centers of many tribal activities today.

Pawhuska is the capital of the Osage Nation, the seat of the tribal government. Pawhuska is a lot like many other towns, with restaurants, stores, schools, and houses.

MAP ILLUSTRATIONS BY GENE THORP, CARTOGRAPHIC CONCEPTS, INC.

This map of the Osage Reservation today includes the three districts, or towns, of Hominy, Grayhorse, and Pawhuska. The town where Christopher lives, Skiatook, sits on the reservation's eastern border, not too far from the city of Tulsa.

The largest and most important Osage gatherings of the year are called the I'n-lon-shka (pronounced: een-LONE-shka) Dances. The dances take place at Hominy, Grayhorse, or Pawhuska for three weekends in a row in June. Osage people who live all over the United States come back to the reservation every year for the dances held in their family's district. The gatherings begin on Thursday and end on Sunday. A lot of people come just to watch, but a lot of people dance, too. Each day, we dance in the afternoon and then take a break for dinner. After we all rest and eat, we start dancing again and continue until about ten or eleven o'clock at night. Because we dance so much during the four days, most Osage people just call the whole event "the dances."

Guests and visitors line up for dinner in Christopher's grandmother's yard.

Since my mom's family is from Pawhuska, we always participate in the dances there. My i'ko lives across the road and down a little way from the dance arbor. Our extended family (sometimes as many as a hundred people, if you include the guests) gathers at her house each evening for a big feast. A lot of different people help prepare the meals. After one of my uncles says a blessing, the dancers usually eat first. That's because, as soon as we finish, we have to start getting dressed in our Osage clothes.

The gatherings at I'ko's house are more than just a time to eat together. Since it's the only time during the year that all of the cousins, aunts, uncles, grandparents, and other family from around the country are together, it's kind of like a big family reunion. If we didn't get together at I'ko's house, I wouldn't know who a lot of my relatives are. I'ko always takes time to recognize family members who have accomplished something big during the past year, or any visitors who have joined us. We also welcome any new babies or people who have married into our family. Usually, there are big cakes to celebrate these special events, and sometimes people give gifts.

Frybread is one of the staples of the family feasts during the I'n-lon-shka Dances. The cooks usually make a couple hundred pieces each night so that there is enough for everyone to eat more than one. Christopher helps to bring the frybread from the kitchen to the serving tables in his i'ko's backyard.

Christopher and his aunt Rox Ann shoo flies away from the platter while his uncle Fred cuts the barbecued chicken into smaller pieces. Other foods on the table include salads, watermelon, vegetables, corn soup, and frybread.

The dance arbor at the village of Grayhorse, as it looked in 1908.
PHOTO BY MARK R. HARRINGTON. (NMAI N2767)

A long time ago Osage dances and ceremonies were held in a wooden structure called a roundhouse (because it was round). Today, the I'n-lon-shka Dances take place under an outdoor arbor. An arbor is a big, permanent metal structure with a roof but no walls. The drum is in the center, surrounded by the drummers, who are men. Around the drummers sit the lady singers who sing with the men. The male dancers sit on benches around the outside edge of the arbor, with those from each district sitting together. Because there are so many dancers, women do not sit on the benches. Instead they enter and leave the dance area for each new song.

Not everyone who attends the I'n-lon-shka is there to dance, but everyone participates in some way. The spectators are usually relatives or friends of the dancers as well as other people from the Osage community. Some people help the dancers get dressed or prepare food for dancers and their families.

An aerial view of the dance arbor (the big building with the blue roof) just before the evening dances begin. Christopher's grandmother's house is in the lower left part of the photo, almost hidden by big trees. PHOTO BY JAMES ELSBERRY (OSAGE), COURTESY OF THE PHOTOGRAPHER.

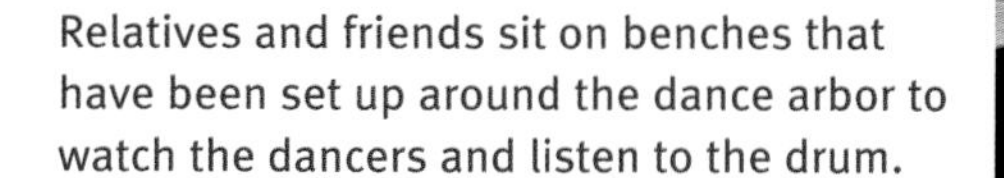

Relatives and friends sit on benches that have been set up around the dance arbor to watch the dancers and listen to the drum.

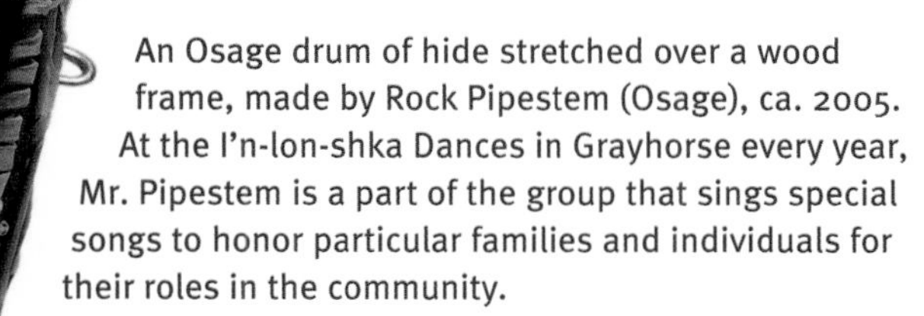

An Osage drum of hide stretched over a wood frame, made by Rock Pipestem (Osage), ca. 2005. At the I'n-lon-shka Dances in Grayhorse every year, Mr. Pipestem is a part of the group that sings special songs to honor particular families and individuals for their roles in the community.

PHOTO BY R. A. WHITESIDE. (NMAI 264575)

The Pawhuska dance arbor at dusk on Saturday night. Christopher and his brothers are inside the arbor dancing.

Osage dancers outside the Grayhorse dance arbor, nearly a hundred years ago.

PHOTO POSTCARD BY VINCE DILLON, 1912. (SMITHSONIAN NATIONAL ANTHROPOLOGICAL ARCHIVES 54,986—COPY OF A PRINT BORROWED FROM THE OSAGE TRIBAL MUSEUM, 1964)

I'n-lon-shka means "playground of the eldest son" in Osage. Both men and women are allowed to dance, but the rules are a little different for each. In order to participate in the dance with the men, boys go through a special ceremony. This includes being given an Osage name, receiving a roach (a headpiece worn by men) and eagle feather, and being welcomed to the community as a new dancer. While girls also receive Osage names, there is no special ceremony or event that welcomes them as dancers. Many girls and women dress in Osage clothing to dance, but many others dance in everyday clothing with just a shawl or blanket wrapped around their shoulders.

PHOTO COURTESY OF KATHRYN RED CORN

LEFT: Christopher at age seven and his brother Geoffrey, with their parents, on the day that the two boys received their roaches and eagle feathers.

RIGHT: Christopher's great-uncle, Charles Red Corn, who gave Christopher his Osage name.

Osage names are usually given by someone from your clan or family. My uncle Charlie gave me my name when I was seven years old. Uncle Charlie is I'ko's older brother. Sometimes names get passed down and sometimes new names are made. I remember that, when I was named, Uncle Charlie called me into the dance arbor and asked me to stand by his side. He took an eagle wing and touched it to my shoulder. Then he said, "This one is Wa-kon-ti-en. It means 'He Walks with God.' This is his name."

I think Wa-kon-ti-en (pronounced: wa-CON-tee-en) is a good name. I like what it means. Uncle Charlie also named my younger brothers. He named Andrew Nu-pat-si (pronounced: new-POT-see), which means "Strength of the Eagle Talon" and David Ma-zhi-nah-tin (pronounced: MA-JHEE-nah-teen), which means "Iron Necklace." Geoffrey's name, Me-ti-onka (pronounced: me-tee-ONKA), means "Playful as the Sun."

After I got my name, I entered the I'n-lon-shka for the first time. Uncle Charlie and the Head Committeeman placed an eagle feather in my roach. The Committeemen are the people in charge of the dances. It is an honored position for men who really know and understand all the traditions of the I'n-lon-shka. I was proud to receive my eagle feather. It meant that I could officially dress in Osage clothes and dance in the I'n-lon-shka with the other Osage men and boys.

Christopher adjusts the eagle feather in his roach.

In many Native communities, an eagle feather that falls to the ground during a dance or ceremony must be retrieved in a special ceremony that purifies, or cleanses, the feather. Often, only certain people are allowed to pick up a fallen feather. Then they may pray over the feather to bless it, or make an offering of tobacco or sweetgrass to show their thanks for the feather and their respect for the strength and dignity of eagles.

Similarly, during the Osage I'n-lon-shka Dances, any part of a dancer's outfit that falls to the ground must be left there. A person called the whipman, who helps the Committeemen keep discipline and order during the dances, picks up the item. Although he doesn't use it today, the whipman carries a braided leather whip to show his position. A dancer who loses any object, including an eagle feather, is required to pay the whipman to get the object back. The amount depends on the importance of what was dropped. The payment reminds dancers that all parts of their clothing are special and should be treated with respect. The whipman is also supposed to make sure that none of the men stay seated during the songs. He does this by dancing in one spot in front of anyone who tries to sit out a song.

Before the dances each night, Christopher's parents make sure that his and his brothers' outfits are fastened securely. When tying the roach to their heads, their dad pulls the long piece of rawhide tight. Sometimes, Christopher says the string leaves marks on his face and chin when he takes it off.

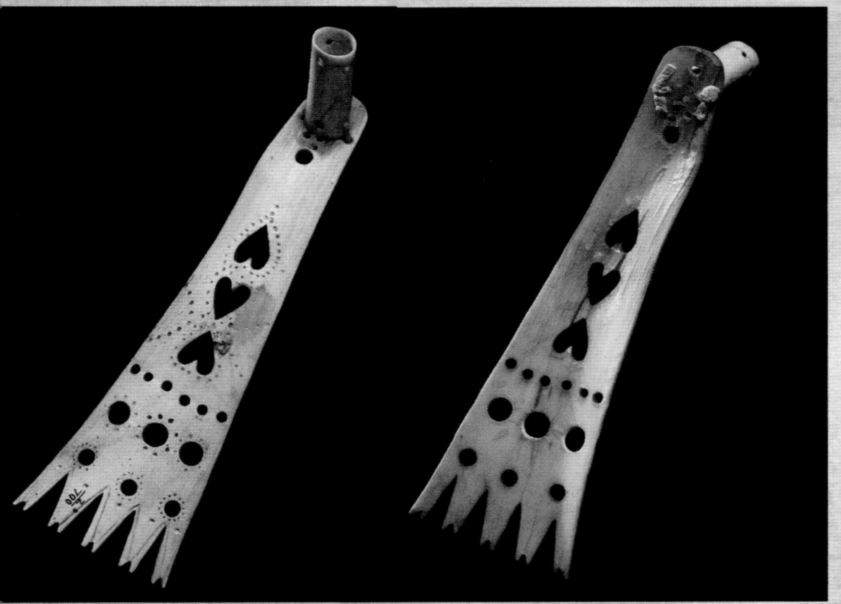

The top and underside of a bone Osage roach spreader. A roach spreader keeps the roach hairs standing upright. The cylinder is placed at the front of the dancer's head to support an eagle feather. Traditionally, a lock of hair from the wearer's head was pulled through the small holes at both ends of the spreader to tie the roach in place. Today, many roach spreaders are made out of German silver and are tied on with string instead of hair. (NMAI 20/700)

Osage people dance in a *straight* style, which means it's not fancy and doesn't involve lots of movement. When we dance, we take small steps in beat with the drum, and most of the movement is from the waist up. We learn to dance by watching others. My uncle Tallee helped me to learn. My brothers and I usually dance with our uncle Tallee and uncle Dickens.

Even though we got our names on the same day, Andrew was too little to start dancing when Geoffrey and I did, but he dances now. In a few years, when David is old enough, my dad, mom, and i'ko will be proud to see all four of us dance together. When it's David's turn to go into the I'n-lon-shka, we will teach him what to do.

When I put on all of my Osage clothes to dance at the I'n-lon-shka, it makes me feel good. I know that participating in the dances helps all of us, old and young, stay connected to our ancestors and our Osage culture. Sometimes when they're talking to the crowd, the Committeemen speak Osage. That makes me feel proud. And since I'm trying to learn the language, I like to listen to what they say.

Christopher, Andrew, and Geoffrey in their grandmother's living room before the dances begin.

David keeps busy playing outside while his older brothers get dressed in their Osage clothes. He will be able to dance with them when he's a few years older.

The inside of the arbor at Pawhuska before the I'n-lon-shka Dances start, June 1980. No one is allowed to take photographs inside the arbor once the dances have begun.
PHOTO BY GLENN WHITE, COURTESY OF THE PHOTOGRAPHER

Many American Indian tribes do not allow pictures to be taken at ceremonies or dances because the ceremonies are sacred or the people do not want outsiders viewing the events. Even though the I'n-lon-shka Dances are not secret or sacred, the Dance Committee decided about forty years ago that no cameras would be allowed inside the arbor during the dances. One of the earliest reasons is that cameras at the time required a flash that used actual light bulbs. When the camera flashed, the bulb would explode, leaving small shards of glass on the ground. This was troublesome for the dancers because, as they moved in a circle around the dirt floor, the broken glass from the flashbulbs would cut the bottoms of their moccasins, which are made out of animal hide. The solution to this problem was to ban cameras under the arbor roof.

As time went by and cameras became more advanced, this type of flashbulb was no longer used, but the Dance Committee decided it was still best not to have cameras. This is because the dances are special and personal to Osage people. Outsiders who take photographs could use them in ways that the people in the photos may not like. Also, sometimes people publish their photos to make money. Since the dances express community and culture, they are not meant to be a source of profit for anyone.

Christopher worries that he might be late because the third bell is ringing. This means that he should be ready in fifteen minutes. Christopher's mom, who is already dressed in her Osage clothes, ties the handkerchief that holds Christopher's otter tail.

If a boy or man isn't wearing his Osage clothes, he won't be allowed to dance. The outfit I wear includes a ribbon shirt, bandolier beads across my shoulders, silver arm bands, a scarf around my neck, breechcloth and hide leggings held up by a wide leather belt, bells around my shins, moccasins, a roach with an eagle feather, and an otter tail down my back. We also carry feather fans because it gets pretty hot in the arbor, especially after we've been dancing for a while!

It usually takes about a half an hour to get dressed, and I always have my dad or mom help me. Since so many people need to get dressed at the same time, not everyone can fit in I'ko's house. A lot of my cousins and uncles get dressed outside, but my brothers and I usually stay inside, where it's not as hot. Getting dressed outside isn't so bad because then you can hear the bell next to the arbor signaling how much more time before the dances will start. There are three bells, and if you're not ready to go to the arbor by the time the third one rings, you'll probably be late! Once we are all dressed, we get together to have a picture taken. Since photos are not allowed at the arbor, we do it at I'ko's house. Then we all walk over to the arbor so that all the men can line up and be seated together. I like the sound that our leg bells make. It's a sound that you only hear during the I'n-lon-shka Dances.

The Town Crier rings the bell to call the dancers to the arbor. It is his job to ring the first bell forty-five minutes before the dances start. This helps the dancers know when to begin getting dressed. All the dancers should be waiting outside the arbor shortly after the third bell rings.

Christopher, his brothers, and some of his cousins have time for a group picture in the side yard of his grandmother's house. Left to right: Christopher's brother Andrew, Christopher, Christopher's brother Geoffrey, Joe Morgan, Jason Darling, Studie Red Corn, Jon Red Corn, Ryan Red Corn, Ben Jacobs, Michael Powell, Jon Jacobs, and Cameron Robinson.

Christopher, two of his brothers, and some of his cousins wait outside the arbor to be escorted to their seats. Left to right: Christopher's younger brother, Andrew; Christopher; his older brother, Geoffrey; and his cousins Joe Morgan, Studie Red Corn, Jon Red Corn, and Ryan Red Corn.

PHOTO BY GENEVIEVE SIMERMEYER

Although Osage clothes don't have any special powers and are not sacred, they do have special meaning. For example, otter tails normally trail behind when you walk. Along with moccasin flaps, the otter tail would in the past have smoothed over any footprints you might have made in the dust, so you would have been harder to track. Today, feather fans help dancers stay cool, but they were also intended to fan away evil spirits. And the bright blue "ghosts" or small bundles that hang from Christopher's bandoliers would in the past have been filled with medicine—such as tobacco, cedar, or flowers—to protect the wearer.

Christopher's roach and eagle feather draped over the arm of the couch. A roach is made of deer hair and the long, soft hairs of a porcupine, which often are dyed bright colors, such as red or purple. Traditionally worn by warriors, the roach represents battle and the smoke of the council fire.

In this painting, an Osage warrior in 1834 wears some of the same clothing Christopher and his brothers wear for the dances today: a roach and eagle feather, silver cuffs, and a feather fan.

GEORGE CATLIN. WA-HO-BÉCK-EE, 1834. OIL ON CANVAS. 73.7 X 60.9 CM. (SMITHSONIAN AMERICAN ART MUSEUM 1985.66.33)

My Osage clothes are not a costume; we call them an outfit or regalia. To me, "costume" means something you dress in to pretend. But I'm not pretending when I dance at the I'n-lon-shka. My outfit is a part of the dance. Dressing in Osage clothes and dancing under the arbor are important parts of who I am as an Osage boy.

Some parts of our outfits can be worn every year, but there are some things that we outgrow, so we need new ones or hand-me-downs. Usually my mom or I'ko makes the new clothes. Sewing a new shirt or moccasins is fairly easy, but other parts of the outfit are more expensive or difficult to make. The roach that I wear belonged to my dad, and my fan is the same one my great-great-grandfather used. As we get older, Geoffrey and I will pass down some of the Osage clothes we wear to Andrew and David.

Folded wool trailer, decorated using a special technique called ribbonwork. A trailer hangs from a dancer's waist, falling behind his back legs nearly to the ground. This one, which includes a lightning-pattern border, was probably made in the early 1900s, but all male I'n-lon-shka dancers still wear them. (NMAI S7529)

All of our Osage clothes are handmade. Normally, aunts, moms, and grandmas sew the outfits for their families. Sometimes, though, there's no one in a family who knows how to make a certain piece. So some people buy parts of their outfits from other Osage people.

From the 1950s to the 1970s, my great-grandma Louise and her sisters Georgeann and Jennie had a store in Pawhuska called the Red Man Store, where people could special-order traditional Osage clothing. A lot of Osage people today are probably still wearing or passing down the clothes from their store! They were especially good at making otter tails, women's skirts and leggings, and the ribbonwork that decorates men's leggings. Ribbonwork involves cutting geometric designs in brightly colored ribbons, which are then sewn on top of each other to make a pattern. Some ribbonwork designs are complicated, so it takes a lot of skill.

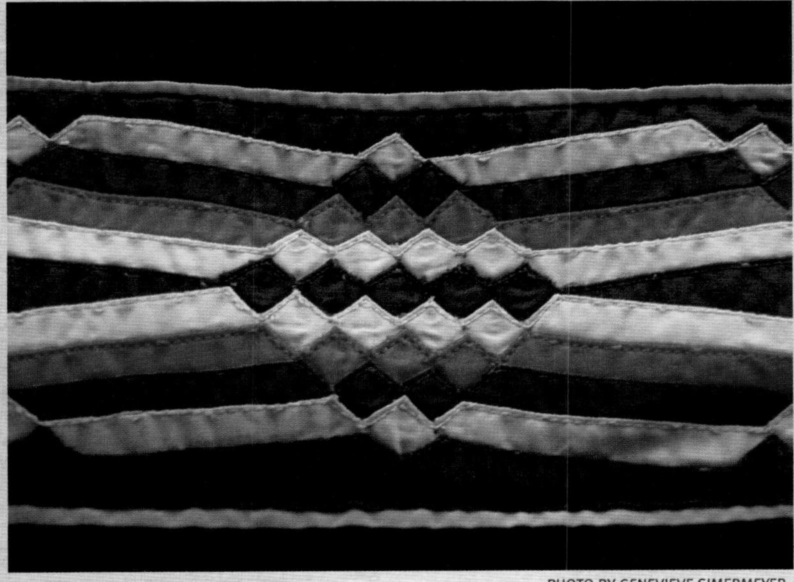

PHOTO BY GENEVIEVE SIMERMEYER

This is a modern wool trailer, decorated with ribbonwork. When French traders brought silk ribbons to trade with Osage people, Osage women cut and sewed the ribbons in designs that had previously been drawn or painted. Some other tribes in the United States make ribbonwork, but Osages are well known for their distinctive designs.

Christopher's mom works on a finger-woven belt. Using a technique similar to braiding, she has to keep track of the order of the yarns and try not to let them get too tangled up.

Christopher and Andrew watch their mother finger weave. So far, she has woven about one foot of a woman's belt. She needs to weave about three more feet before the belt will be done. The belt is about seven or eight inches wide.

Finger weaving is another skill that provides an important part of our outfits. Finger weaving is a technique of weaving brightly colored strands of yarn together to make a woman's belt, a sash, or garters, which are used by men and women to hold up leggings. It's a slow process, so it can take a long time to make a whole belt, for example. The patterns of arrows or chevrons are made by looping the different colors over and under each other, using just your fingers. The designs are always symmetrical, so you have to start in the middle and work out to the left and right to make sure it's all the same. My mom is a really good finger weaver. She ties the yarn around an old highchair so that she can pull the belt straight in front of her as she weaves. She's started to teach me how to do it, but so far I've made only a small garter.

Chris in his i'ko's yard after the dancing has ended for the evening, watching a sparkler burn itself out on a piece of sheet metal.

I have so much fun during the dances. I get to stay up late, sleep outside, eat lots of good food, and play with all of my cousins and brothers. Sometimes, on Saturday night after we're all done dancing, my dad and uncles let us play with sparklers. If we're lucky, they might even shoot off a few big fireworks out in the field behind I'ko's house! I love seeing the explosions of colored sparks in the dark sky.

There's always so much going on during the weekend of the dances. I know that it takes a lot of time to get everything ready, but the effort is always worth it. When I think about it, the I'n-lon-shka Dances celebrate one big Osage family. We feed each other, we clothe each other, and we celebrate together. Like other families, we like to share with those around us. And for me, this means sharing Osage ways. So whether I am at school, church, or Scouts, I am proud to be who I am—and to let others know it.

Pah-me-she-wah, whose name in English was Tresa Bigheart, with her baby. This is a formal studio portrait with a classical painted backdrop, and Mrs. Bigheart is wearing traditional Osage clothing.

Clarence L. Tinker, who became a major general in the Army Air Corps. Tinker was killed in 1942 in an airplane crash during the Battle of Midway. Tinker Field, near Oklahoma City, was named for him. Every year at the I'n-lon-shka Dances in Pawhuska, a special song is sung in memory of his distinguished military service.

Emma Strikeaxe. With her pina style dress and huge hair ribb Emma is dressed in fancy "mo clothes of the era.

A little over one hundred years ago, the United States government made a list of 2,229 names. These were names of old people and young people, men and women, parents and children. The document changed the lives of everyone listed, and even today it remains significant.

There are many reasons that the United States made this list. It had to do with where and how people could live. But most significantly, it was a list of Osage people. Every Osage person born by June 30, 1907, had his or her name on the list. They were the citizens of the Osage Nation.

Vernie L. Hutchinson Akin, with five puppies—and a big flower attached to her headband.

The people on that list were very diverse. Some lived modern lives, while others followed old ways. Many spoke only Osage, but many had learned to speak English, French, or other tribal languages. Throughout their lives many would own cars and some would pilot airplanes. At the same time, some of the people never wore anything but traditional Osage clothing and lived only in traditional Osage dwellings. On the list were doctors, politicians, teachers, engineers, and musicians. Some of the men were traditional warriors, and others served in the United States military. But no matter who these Osage people were or how they lived their lives, they are our ancestors. And they are important to all of their descendants.

ames, whose Osage name was Kah-he-ah-gra,
s wife, Minnie Harvey James. Her Osage name was
-to-me. He is dressed in a suit and tie, while Mrs.
is dressed in Osage clothing. She wears a large
work blanket and a set of silver brooches called
a pins.

E-to-moie, whose name in English means "Little Star." He wears a hat made of otter fur, traditionally worn by Osage warriors.

George Connor.

Adelia Edna Connor Revard Ladd. Her haircut, lipstick, and fur collar give her a glamorous 1920s look.

John Claremore and his children.

Louis Claremore, whose Osage name was Tsa-pah-ke-ah. This baby is dressed in a lace-trimmed, sailor-style suit.

Anna Miles Froe (Mo-se-che-he) and Mary Miles Crowther Schoonover (Wah-shah-ah-pe), standing on the porch of their home.

Rose Little Star Tohee

John Oberly, whose Osage name was Le-ta-man-ze. Mr. Oberly was the brother of Christopher's great-great-grandmother, Jennie Garfield Gray, who is pictured on page 7. He became chief of the Osage Nation in 1949 and served in this position until his death in 1951. In this photo, he wears a shirt, scarf, beads, trailer, and moccasins that are very similar to the clothing Christopher wears in the dances today.

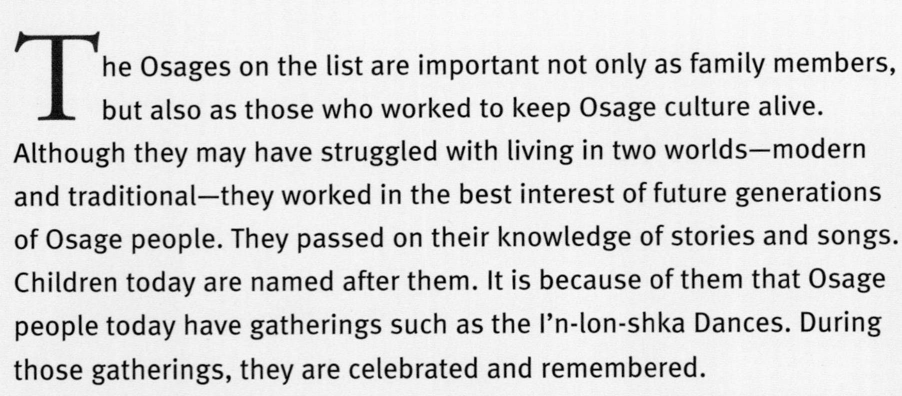

The Osages on the list are important not only as family members, but also as those who worked to keep Osage culture alive. Although they may have struggled with living in two worlds—modern and traditional—they worked in the best interest of future generations of Osage people. They passed on their knowledge of stories and songs. Children today are named after them. It is because of them that Osage people today have gatherings such as the I'n-lon-shka Dances. During those gatherings, they are celebrated and remembered.

The photographs on these three pages are pictures of some of those people. Each portrait shows how these different Osage people saw themselves. The clothing, hairstyles, and settings show that Osage people, each in his or her own way, lived in the old and new.

Josephine Claremore Walker and Elizabeth Pitts. The girls are wearing Osage clothing and jewelry, including multi-stranded bead necklaces and round, silver *wabaka* pins at their throats, yet they are standing in a traditional Victorian room with bookshelves and a Persian rug. Today, women dress in similar shirts and jewelry for the I'n-lon-shka Dances.